Dear Shirley —

God Bless you!

Arne Vick

HOW TO SIT IN CHURCH AND GET NOTHING...

HOW TO SIT IN CHURCH AND GET NOTHING...

This book may be ordered from:

Arne Vick
8811 Canoga Avenue No. 303
Canoga Park, California 91304

DEDICATED
TO MY WIFE
MARTHA

Who has been a rare and delightful
companion on life's ever-changing
road.   Til Sammen i Himlen!

CONTENTS

PREFACE

In a wide-ranging ministry covering two-thirds
of my lifetime and five continents, there have
been those who would occasionally ask, "Do
you have anything in print?" Hitherto the reply has had to be negative, but with the publi-
cation of this little compilation the "No" is
changed to "Yes."
May that which is stated of "He that prophe-
cieth" in I Corinthians 14:3 find some parallel
in these written pages. May they also minister,
"edification, and exhortation, and comfort."

HOW TO SIT IN CHURCH AND
GET NOTHING

It is entirely possible to sit in a fine restaurant and starve to death! A table laden with good food cannot prevent starvation! Certain basic requirements must be met by the diner before nourishment, pleasure, and satisfaction of the available food can be his. Simple yet essential attitudes and actions, involving varying degrees of effort, are required before food on the table can become food in the stomach—with its resultant benefits.

In the simplest terms these steps can be described as *appropriation*, reaching out to convey food to the mouth; *mastication*, chewing food in preparation for swallowing; and *assimilation* through proper digestion.

13

All of this provides a valid spiritual analogy. To sit in church and starve spiritually is a tragically common experience. To sit in God's house, hearing God's Word, sensing God's presence, without inwardly responding and reaching out to appropriate the available grace and blessing, is nothing less than tragic.

The average churchgoer having this experience usually blames the preacher for his failure to receive soul food, thus revealing his ignorance of the fact that every sermon has two ends: the preacher and the hearer! To this truth the Scripture gives absolute support: "The word preached did not profit them, not being mixed with faith in them that heard." The preacher must come into his pulpit fully prepared in both head and heart. Equally important, the hearer must listen to God's Word with an open heart, a willing mind, and a right spirit.

Jesus taught the necessity of spiritual response, saying, "But whereunto shall I liken this generation? It is like unto children sitting in the markets, and calling unto their fellows, and saying, we have piped unto you, and ye have not danced" (Matthew 11:16, 17). As response to the rhythm of the music is essential to the dancer, so inward response (involving unreserved acceptance of and submission to God's Word) is mandatory if the preached Word is to become bread for the soul.

How to sit in church and get nothing is plainly shown in the Scriptures:

1. *Listen with a critical spirit* as the Pharisees in Luke 11:53, 54: "Seeking to catch something out of his mouth, that they might accuse him." A critical attitude in church closes the mind, the heart, and the soul of the hearer. It effectively prevents the entrance of the Word for it is a deliberate and rebellious rejection of the divine exhortation: "Receive with meekness of the engrafted word." Or, as the Amplified New Testament has it, "In a humble spirit receive and welcome the Word."

Our personal disapproval of the preacher in no way removes our responsibility to the message! The Scripture abounds in examples of unworthy vessels being used of God to convey His will and transmit His Word. For the genuine Christian there is but one acceptable attitude in church: "Speak, Lord, for thy servant heareth" (1 Samuel 3:9).

2. *Listen with a superior attitude* as did the proud Athenians to Paul in the marketplace: "What will this babbler say?" (Acts 17:18). Their scornful words fully revealed their inflated opinion of their own superiority. What mockery the centuries have made of them! Paul's work has never died—through his divinely inspired epistles he continues to influence the minds and lives of millions—while the anonymous philosophers of Athens who ridiculed him are long since forgotten.

To sit in church with a feeling of superiority toward God's minister is to guarantee a futile and disappointing service.

3. *Listen with a sophisticated and know-it-all attitude* like the Pharisees when the healed blind man tried to give them his testimony:

"Thou wast altogether born in sins, and dost thou teach us?" (John 9:34). They were outraged that one so obviously untutored and unpolished should dare to reason with them concerning spiritual things. And they were blindly unaware of the principle stated by Jesus in His exultant prayer, "I thank thee, O Father, Lord of heaven and earth, that thou hast hid these things from the wise and prudent, and hast revealed them unto babes" (Luke 10:21).

It is cause for concern if a church refuses to consider a pastoral candidate unless he holds a college degree. Such thinking is a sad departure from Paul's triumphant declaration of God-sufficiency: "But God hath chosen the foolish things of the world to confound the wise; and God hath chosen the weak things to confound the things which are mighty . . . that no flesh should glory in his presence."

Perhaps we should carefully ponder the words of the famous J. H. Jowett: "It is the child-spirit that approaches life's golden gates and finds them all ajar. The proudly aggressive in spirit, contending for place and power, may force many a door, but they are not doors that open into enduring wealth and peace. Real inheritance becomes ours only through humility. The lowly make great discoveries; to them the earth is full of God's glory."

4. *Listen with bored indifference* like the sons-in-law of Lot when he tried to warn them of Sodom's impending doom: "Up, get you out of this place, for the Lord will destroy this city. But he seemed as one that mocked unto his sons-in-law" (Genesis 19:14). Theirs was a common contemporary attitude; a stubborn, sometimes sullen, refusal to hear and accept any message that warns or calls for effort and action.

While all God's prophets were often ignored and reviled, defied and despised, Jeremiah stands out for the intensity of vituperation he endured, for the fury of opposition he encountered, and the mulish recalcitrance of his hearers. He described the unteachable attitudes of some of them: "They have made their faces harder than a rock; they have refused to return. . . . I spoke unto you, rising up early and speaking unto you, but ye heard not; I called you, but ye answered not" (Jeremiah 5:3; 7:13).

The wise Christian diligently avoids falling into any of these negative and potentially destructive attitudes, remembering that "the rebellious dwell in a dry land" (Psalm 68:6). Rather, his constant delight is in the law of the Lord, and he finds his true attitude expressed in Jeremiah 15:16: "Thy words were found, and I did eat them, and thy word was unto me the joy and the rejoicing of mine heart."

CHOOSING THE RIGHT CHURCH

If the apostle Paul were alive today on earth, which church would he join?

He certainly would have a· wide selection of churches from which to choose. Statistics indicate the existence of approximately 250 separate denominations or organized groups of professing Christians in America. It is almost inevitable that one should be confused and bewildered when he tries to decide which of the multitudinous claimants to heaven's approval actually presents the strongest case in the light of God's Word.

If the inquirer will subject all denominational claims to authenticity to the test of the Scriptures, he soon will find his confusion giving way to solid conviction. In the case of Paul, we know by his epistles that he arrived at a very certain decision as to the kind of church God intended His people to have.

A careful study of Paul's epistles will yield an answer both clear and accurate to the question, "Which is the right church?" He has forever gone on record—in language sometimes thunderous, always unmistakable—as to his position on the great doctrines of the gospel of Christ. No human autobiography ever written can surpass in self-revelation the epistles of Paul. They are unsparing. His extreme God-consciousness during the actual writing or dictating of them comes through in such statements as, "I say the truth in Christ, I lie not, my conscience also bearing me witness in the Holy Ghost" (Romans 9:1); "We speak before God in Christ . . ." (2 Corinthians 12:19); and, "In the sight of God speak we in Christ" (2 Corinthians 2:17).

It can most certainly be assumed that, in his search for a church home today, Paul would not be much influenced in his decision to join because of its size, its modern facilities, its prominent location, its program, or its prestige. Nor would the personal qualities of its pastor— his personality, his education, age, ability, nor his popularity—have any appreciable bearing on Paul's decision. The choice would be determined basically by the faithfulness of both the pastor and the church to the truth of God's Word, and his overriding desire would be to find and fellowship with those of "like precious faith."

19

What, then, would be the great foundation truths that Paul would demand as part of the teaching and practice of *his* church? For the answers we turn to his own writings in his letters to the churches of his day. The following order of listing does not necessarily reflect the relative importance of each truth.

First, Paul's church must *accept the Bible as the infallible and divinely inspired Word of God.*

This major truth was cherished by the apostle to the very end of his life, for it is in the second letter to Timothy—the last of all his epistles, written in the shadow of the executioner ("I am now ready to be offered . . .") —that he records for all generations to follow his unshakable opinion of the Holy Scriptures: "All scripture is given by inspiration of God . ." (2 Timothy 3:16). If Paul were here today he would be shocked to discover the incredible inroads of liberalism against his declared concept of the divine inspiration of the Scriptures, and he would be disturbed to find that masses of professing Christians experience varying degrees of doubt as to their ultimate authority in things relating to both time and eternity.

With all such doubt-plagued, vacillating, and uncertain souls he would find himself sadly out of step and without any feeling of spiritual *rapport,* with its consequent desire for increasing identification and affiliation. *His* church *must* agree with his unshakable affirmation, "All scripture is given by inspiration of God!"

Again, *Paul's church must accept Christ as the uniquely divine, virgin-born, eternally existent, Son of God.*

From his inspired pen often flowed such rapturous peans of praise and sublime exaltations of Jesus as the Christ, God's only begotten Son, that human language could scarce support it. We need but to consider one passage from his epistles to be instantly immersed in and exhilarated by his breath-taking *magnificat*. Here are some phrases from Paul's pen in the first chapter of the Colossian letter: "For by him were all things created. . . ." "He is before all things, and by him all things consist." "For it pleased the Father that in him should all fulness dwell" (Colossians 1:16, 17, 19).

Any person with such a concept of the identity of Jesus of Nazareth would never apply for membership in a church where Christ was reduced to the category of a mere human teacher and religious leader. Paul would undoubtedly reject fellowship with all such, saying, "For in him dwelleth all the fulness of the Godhead bodily."

Furthermore, the *church of Paul's choice must be a fellowship of born-again believers*—individuals who have an experiential, heartfelt, life-transforming knowledge of God through Jesus Christ.

For he who wrote, "If any man be in Christ, he is a new creature . . ." (2 Corinthians 5:17), could never identify himself with a congrega-

21

tion of people who were personally ignorant of the true meaning of the "new birth" and whose concept of Christianity consisted of mere intellectual assent to the gospel story—with an added veneer of outward righteousness. To such misguided people Paul would constantly reiterate, "They that are in the flesh cannot please God" (Romans 8:8), and "By grace are ye saved through faith; and that not of yourselves: it is the gift of God: not of works, lest any man should boast" (Ephesians 2:8, 9).

In fact, it is highly doubtful whether Paul would consent to the use of the word "church" in speaking of certain groups of alleged followers of Christ today. An "audience" is not necessarily a "congregation," in the scriptural sense of the world, any more than a "crowd" constitutes a "church." For only to those who gather together in His name, though they be but two or three in number, is the promise of Jesus' presence given. Paul would insist that the meetings of his church be spiritual in atmosphere and be characterized by worship "in spirit and in truth."

Moreover, it is clearly seen from Paul's writings that his concept of the church *included the provision that its members must be Spirit-filled and recipients of "the promise of the Father"*—the baptism in the Holy Spirit—which was first given at Jerusalem on the day of Pentecost.

For in the epistle generally rated the most profoundly spiritual of all his letters, he fervently exhorts—yea, commands—the Christians of Ephesus to "be filled with the Spirit" (Ephesians 5:18). Just what would be his opinion of the average denominational church of today, with its rejection of the baptism of the Spirit according to the apostolic pattern of Acts 2:4, and its consequent failure to receive and exercise the gifts of the Spirit?

All the evidence in both the Book of Acts and the epistles that follow leads to the clear conclusion that the early Christians were *all* Spirit-filled, taking their standard from the pattern established on the Day of Pentecost when "they were *all* filled with the Holy Ghost, and began to speak with other tongues, as the Spirit gave them utterance" (Acts 2:4). Paul's intense desire that believers should go on beyond conversion to receive the baptism of the Spirit is plainly seen in his immediate and searching query of the disciples at Ephesus, "Have ye received the Holy Ghost since ye believed?" (Acts 19:2). How the man who could write without the slightest reticence, for the Christian church of all ages to read, "I thank my God, I speak with tongues more than ye all" (1 Corinthians 14:18), could ever bring himself to affiliate with a church that rejected both the scripturalness and the importance of this Pentecostal experience, is impossible to conceive.

That Paul was also a firm believer in *physical healing through prayer*, and that he practiced the same continually, is a matter of abundant record.

He experienced his first personal healing within hours after his Damascus road conversion when, in his blinded state, he heard Ananias say, "Brother Saul, the Lord, even Jesus . . . hath sent me that thou mayest receive thy sight . . . and immediately there fell from his eyes as it had been scales: and he received sight forthwith . . ." (Acts 9:17, 18).

This personal miracle, so early in his new life, must have played a large part in the formulating of future faith and practice; and thereafter, throughout his long and fruitful ministry, God honored his faith "with signs following." The Bible says, "And God wrought special miracles by the hands of Paul" (Acts 19:11). It describes the healing of the life-long cripple at Lystra, recorded in Acts 14:8-10, plus many other miracles on Paul's missionary travels. The apostle sums these up in 2 Corinthians 12:12 saying, "Truly the signs of an apostle were wrought among you in all patience, in signs, and wonders, and mighty deeds."

In the light of all this, simple logic demands the conclusion that Paul's church today must preach and practice divine healing.

In the theology of Paul one further major truth shines through with throbbing hope and radiant expectation—*the return of Jesus, "to be glorified in his saints, and to be admired in all them that believe . . ."* (2 Thessalonians 1:10).

In fact, it is to Paul that we are indebted for the greater portion of our knowledge of this transcendent event. How greatly impoverished we would be if Paul had not given us 1 Thessalonians 4:13-18, which opens with the familiar, "But I would not have you to be ignorant, brethren, concerning them which are asleep"—which reaches its awesome climax with the apocalyptic unveiling, "For the Lord himself shall descend from heaven with a shout."

And what a tremendous gap would exist in our understanding of God's end-time purposes if we had been deprived of Paul's revelation in 1 Corinthians 15:51-54, opening with the soul-thrilling announcement, "Behold, I show you a mystery; we shall not all sleep, but we shall all be changed." Certainly Paul would not seek membership in any church today that did not accept and live in the light of our Lord's glorious return. These are but two of many passages in Paul's writings which testify to his total commitment to the truth of Christ's return; and again, we are forced to conclude that any church hoping to include him among its members must share his views on this subject also.

All students of the Pauline epistles will instantly be reminded of many other great truths given the Church through the apostle, and the present writer is well aware of them all. He has no thought of ignoring or modifying Paul's emphasis on such vital truths as sanctification, the fruit of the Spirit, death to the old nature, and many more. But these and related subjects fall generally into the area of spiritual growth and achievement of Christian maturity, whereas the object of this article has been to discover the foundational truths of the Early Church that we might find a Bible answer to the question, "Which is the right church?"

TRUTH OR CONSEQUENCES

Have you ever played "Truth or Consequences"? There is a popular radio program by that name, and when a contestant gives a wrong answer the man in charge says, "You haven't told the truth, so you must take the consequences." In a sense, every one of us is playing that game, for God has established it as a basic principle of life that if we do not tell the truth we must take the consequences. The consequences of lying are inescapable, not only as regards future judgment but also in this present life.

When thinking of the evils of lying we are prone to recall the drastic penalty inflicted upon Ananias and Sapphira in the Early Church, and perhaps secretly thank God that

27

such severe measures are not commonly used by Him today. We mistakenly feel that if adversity, scandal, and shame do not follow our falsehoods we have escaped judgment and have "gotten away with it."

But this is pure delusion, for the "consequences" will immediately appear *within!* The inward penalty of lying is the instant loss of a good conscience, the forfeiture of peace of mind, the fear of exposure, the sacrifice of self-respect, and an inevitable weakening of one's moral fiber, leading to subtle undermining of character and personality. Thus, "telling the truth or taking the consequences" becomes a literal and unavoidable choice, affecting the whole man, physically, mentally, morally, and spiritually.

That Christians are capable of lying is plainly shown by Paul's exhortation to the Ephesian church: "Wherefore putting away lying, speak every man truth with his neighbour." But the incongruity of the thought is repulsive—how can lying lips be found in the person who professes to be indwelt by the One who said, "I am . . . the truth," and by the Holy Ghost, who is called "the Spirit of truth"?

However, the incidence of brazen falsehood is relatively rare among Christians. Among believers the menace takes on far more subtle aspects. For here the lie must be camouflaged by a measure of truth to make it reasonably tolerable to the conscience, much as the pill is sugar-coated to make it palatable and to hide

28

its bitter ingredients. Thus the "half-truth" and the "slight exaggeration" come into common usage, without seemingly causing the slightest disturbance to the conscience of the offender. But there is no verbal "twilight zone" where matters are neither light nor dark, neither true nor false. White is white and black is black. Truth is truth and lying is lying! And that which is not *all* the truth really is not the truth at all! "Wherefore putting away lying, speak every man truth with his neighbour" (Eph. 4:25).

Handling the truth is like handling money; absolute *honesty* and integrity must prevail. And be assured that God's standards are not relative. We would not dream of speaking of a "little adultery" or a "little murder"; yet we speak of "little lies," when actually the latter is as impossible as the former. The man who steals a dime is as much a thief as the man who steals a million dollars. And the man who deliberately departs from the truth in the least is actually as much a liar as the most shameless prevaricator. In both cases it is the violation of principle rather than the degree of transgression that determines guilt.

This also the Master made clear—"He that is unjust in the least is unjust also in much." Thus, if a man says he pays his tithes when he knows that at the end of the year he has given less than one-tenth of his income to God, he is guilty of sin. And if a pastor states that his church seats a thousand people when he knows that it actually seats only seven hundred, he is a liar by God's definition. Or if an evangelist knowingly and with intent to deceive boasts an audience of two thousand, when by actual count there are less than twelve hundred chairs available, he also exercises "lying lips."

The Christian who can thus handle the truth carelessly and feel that it is of small significance whether or not he exercises absolute honesty in speech, is self-revealed as one who has never had a true revelation of God's white-hot holiness such as we find presented in Revelation 20:11: "And I saw a great white throne, and him that sat on it, from whose face the earth and heaven fled away; and there was found no place for them." Nor does such a one walk with a daily sense of God's all-seeing eye upon him as did Paul. "But as of sincerity, but as of God, in the sight of God speak we in Christ" (2 Corinthians 2:17). Mark the sober words, "In the sight of God speak we."

Both God's estimation of lying and the terrifying ultimate "consequences" thereof are set forth in the Revelation in language most awesome and terrible. The man with callous conscience concerning careful conversation needs but to meditate with open mind on Revelation 21:8 and 22:15, to be forever jolted out of his deadly complacency. "All liars shall have their part in the lake which burneth with fire and brimstone." "For without [the gates of heaven] are . . . murderers, and idolaters, and whosoever loveth and maketh a lie!"

UNSAID AND UNDONE

Regret, in some measure, must be present at the death of every human being. Not only regret over wrongs done, but far more for good undone. For in every person's mind there is a backlog of duties unperformed, of obligations ignored, of responsibilities neglected. The universal tendency to put off action on vital matters traps us into inaction until often it becomes too late.

Our *intentions* are good and praiseworthy but so few of them are carried out. Thus, the husband who actually has a genuine and deep devotion for his wife, and who in solitary moments of contemplation realizes with a rush of gratitude just how much she really means to him, will make a mental note to tell her of his sincere affection and esteem; but somehow the right moment never seems to come. So the sweet and loving words that would have meant so much to her are never spoken, until one day he gazes with tear-blinded eyes and anguished heart at her dear face as it lies in the coffin. *Then* the full realization of his loss strikes him and *then* he brokenly sobs out the words of love and appreciation—but too late!

Thus also, the wife with a faithful and devoted husband will often think in the quiet hours of his goodness and his labor and toil to provide the necessities of life for his family, and she will promise herself that she will not fail to *tell* him all that she feels for him. But that right moment never seems to come, so they continue going through life side by side, both hungering to exchange words of love and esteem for one another but neither doing so. And so it is in all of life's relationships; we leave unsaid that which would mean so much if it were only said, between husband and wife, children and parents, pastor and people, employer and employee. *"Do it now"* is a motto that would revolutionize a thousand relationships in a moment, if it were applied to the backlog of our good intentions.

And if the foregoing be true of the unsaid, what shall we say concerning the great undone in every life? "One of these days I'm going to . . . " is a universal habit. Latin America may be characterized as "The land of *mañana*"—"The land of tomorrow." The attitude of its people may be, "Never do today what you can put off until tomorrow." But the spiritual philosophy of *"mañana"* is not confined to any one part of the earth. The woman of Samaria (John 4) is seen as one of its devotees when she exclaimed to Christ, "I know that Messias cometh . . . ; when He is come, He will tell us all things." If she possessed that Messianic knowledge why was she living as she was? Obviously it was due to a misguided notion that in the dim, distant future, when Messiah came, He would by a flick of His divine wrist transform her sinfulness into holiness, her squalid uncleanness into immaculate purity. Her *present* was a "mess" concerning which she had been unwilling to take any action for improvement, but her future she pictured in rosy hues, when the Messiah would do some miraculous work for her.

But how abruptly the Master shattered her false hopes and brought her out of the dream world of *"mañana"* into the ever present reality of *now* with His startling announcement, *"I that speak unto thee am He!"* In her sordid life the *undone* ran headon into the demands of the *now*.

This woman of Sychar is a perfect example of multitudes of people today. They recognize, and in moments of spiritual honesty they may even admit (to themselves, at least) that their present life is far from what it *ought to be*. But the necessary corrections are constantly postponed; the *undone* pyramids and accumulates more and more. The required consecration or confession or restitution is not made and so the spiritual life continues to sag, lag, and drag along, without victory or satisfaction. But always there is the dim hope and pledge that on some distant tomorrow life will suddenly become all that it *should be* and all that we *desire* it to be. The delusion persists that the overcoming power, the abundant grace, and the spiritual glory so sadly lacking now will burst upon us with cataclysmic radiance *then*.

All such thinking is but sheer spiritual daydreaming and produces nothing—"The soul of the sluggard desireth and hath nothing" (Prov. 13:4). The spiritual sluggard "hath nothing" because he will "do nothing." But the scripture continues to state that "The soul of the diligent shall be made fat." The diligent soul *does something* and gets results—is "made fat." The modern "sluggard" might be called a "tramp." Even a tramp can *"desire"* a better life, but it will never be his until he forsakes the rut of "do-nothing" and begins to take diligent action towards his goal.

This human tendency to dream about tomorrow instead of living in today is also seen in Martha, the sister of Lazarus. When Jesus stood before the grave and said, "Thy brother shall rise again," she immediately projected the promised miracle into the sweet by-and-by of the last day. But Christ had said nothing about the last day, and He corrected her erroneous attitude by stating, "I *am* the resurrection and

34

the life." He seemed to say, "If I am able to raise Lazarus on the last day, I am able to raise him now, for I am the '*I Am*' and not the '*I will be*'." And having said this He proceeded to give a living demonstration of His own teaching and practice.

The attitude shown by Martha on this occasion is widespread today. The sinner will not accept salvation now, but he secretly expects to make his peace with God on the last day—his last day on earth. Young people are often annoyed when pressed to serve Christ; they say, "I'm too young to become serious about religion; later in life, when I am ready to settle down, *then* I'll become a Christian." Lukewarm Christians promise themselves that "one of these days" they are going to get down to business and really pray through and get the Fire once again. Backsliders always plan to return to the fold "some day," but a convenient season never seems to come. And thus procrastination continues to reap its deadly harvest while golden opportunities are lost that may never return —opportunities for service to God and man, for a richer Christian life, for a more victorious experience in grace.

We forget that the *right thing* can be done at the *wrong time* and thereby lose its value completely. Judas Iscariot is a solemn example of this. Matthew 27 reveals that he fulfilled three of the chief requirements for salvation, but *too late*. He exercised *repentance* ("when he saw that He was condemned, repented himself," v. 3). He performed *restitution* ("he brought again the thirty pieces of silver to the chief priests and elders," v. 3), and he made *confession* ("saying, I have sinned in that I have betrayed the innocent blood," v. 4). Yet all these highly commendable words and deeds, though performed with the utmost sincerity, could not undo his wicked deed. It was too late!

Days become weeks, weeks become years, and still the twin pyramids called *unsaid* and *undone* continue to grow rather than diminish in most lives. Finally death comes, as it must to all, and at its dread approach the mind at last awakens regarding these matters. In tragic retrospect, and with penetrating insight of self that comes only on eternity's border, it realizes that now at last thère remains *no more time* to be wasted. Then comes the pathetic and fruitless wishing for another opportunity to clear up some of the backlog of the *unsaid* and the *undone*. And thus, to repeat our opening sentence, "Regret, in some measure, must be present at the death of every human being." Therefore, whatever we *ought* to say or do, let us *do it now*.

STRONG CRYING AND TEARS

Prayer runs the gamut from adoring whispers to torrential outpourings of verbal lava. Between these two extremes prayer can be calm and comforting, intelligent and eloquent, routine and heart-warming. Prayer can be praise or thanksgiving; supplication or intercession. It can be soundless, as was Hannah's; and it can be wordless, as was the sinner woman's who washed His feet with her tears.

But there is also another kind of prayer that is distinctive in its unrelenting concentration on one specific object and request. Such was the prayer of Elijah in his seven-time supplication for rain, and such was the prayer of Jesus in Gethsemane, of which the record states, "He prayed *the third time, saying the same words*" (Matthew 26:44). It seems certain that Hebrews 5:7 refers to Jesus' experience in the Garden: "Who in the days of his flesh . . . offered up prayers with strong crying and tears. . . ."

While there is no passage of Scripture to support any idea that all of Jesus' praying was of this nature, yet it clearly shows there were occasions when His praying was marked by extreme intensity and profound emotional involvement!

It seems to me that this kind of praying has become increasingly and regrettably more scarce in recent years. Granted that *loud praying,* per se, has no Bible premium placed upon it and can actually be as distasteful—and futile —as the Pharisees *long praying.* Granted that the decibel output of the supplicant's voice can not necessarily be equated with spiritual power. The stubborn fact remains that a human being in extreme distress—whether threatened with drowning, trapped in a burning building, or lost in a forest—never carefully modulates his voice when crying for help!

That there exists a clear relationship between the degree of feeling within and the sound of the voice is not hard to establish. When Jesus stood before the tomb of Lazarus, the Scripture states that He "cried with a loud voice, Lazarus, come forth." Certainly it was not for the sake of Lazarus that Jesus' voice was loud, for the loudest voice cannot alone awake the dead. I believe it was due to the tremendous surge of divine power that swept up and out of His innermost being and was transmitted to the dead man by and through His words, "Lazarus, come forth!"

In our understandably negative reaction to incidents and individuals that have seemed to violate the Bible rule, "Let all things be done decently and in order" (1 Corinthians 14:40), we should beware lest we over-react and muzzle genuine travail, stifle spontaneity, quench Holy Ghost praying, and place our people in spiritual straitjackets. This is not intended as a defense of unseemly screaming, yelling, or bellowing, but simply a plea for the true liberty of the Spirit in our prayer meetings and at our altar services. The very real danger is that we destroy the wheat with the tares.

We Pentecostals who claim the identical experience enjoyed by the Christians in the Book of Acts, have a unique responsibility to validate our claim by duplicating their record. Most of our concepts of the church in its daily life and activities are drawn from the Acts. This should most certainly include their practice and methods of prayer.

While several detailed descriptions of apostolic prayer meetings can be found in the Book of Acts, perhaps the most impressive is the report of the occasion of which it is recorded, "When they had prayed, the place was shaken where they were assembled" (Acts 4:31). Some of the newer translations use even stronger language, "The place where they were was violently moved"; "the place in which they had gathered rocked to and fro"; and, "their meeting place shook."

Is it possible to imagine a prayer meeting that produced such a result could have been marked by a hushed and funereal atmosphere, by general inhibition and restraint, by painful pauses and solemn silences? Hardly, when the record plainly tells us that "they lifted up their voice to God with one accord" (Acts 4:24). Two facts clearly emerge: (1) they prayed *in unison;* (2) *they prayed aloud.*

Such a prayer meeting might have greatly pleased the celebrated Baptist preacher, Charles Spurgeon. For surprising though it may be, Spurgeon chided the Methodists of his day for their loss of glory and freedom in prayer. The following ringing plea is from the pen of the eloquent preacher himself:

"How I delight to listen to a brother who talks to God simply and from his heart; and I must confess I have no small liking to those rare old-fashioned Methodist prayers, which are now quite out-of-date.

"Our Methodist friends, for the most part, are getting too fine and respectable nowadays; too genteel to allow of prayers such as once made the walls to ring and ring again. Oh, for a revival of those glorious, violent prayers which flew like hot shot against the battlements of heaven (Matthew 11:12).

40

"Oh, for more moving of the posts of the doors *in vehemence;* more thundering at the gates of mercy! I would sooner attend a prayer meeting where there were *groans and cries all over the place,* and shouts of hallelujah! than be in your polite assemblies where everything is dull as death and decorous as the white-washed sepulchre!

"Oh, for more of the power of God; the body, soul, and spirit working together, *the whole man being aroused and startled up to the highest pitch of intensity*—to wrestle with the Most High.

"Such, I have no doubt, the prayer of Jesus was on the cold mountainside." (Italics mine.)

Brethren, if the Baptist Spurgeon, long decades before the Latter Rain outpouring, could express his feelings about prayer, with such potent words as *violent vehemence, thundering, groans, cries, shouts, aroused,* and *intensity,* how can we possibly fear them?

What glorious revivals, what profound renewals, what transformations in individuals and churches would ensue if the situation described in Judges 21:2 were to be reenacted in every Assembly of God across the nation. "And *the people came* to the house of God, *and abode there* till even before God, and *lifted up their voices,* and *wept sore."*

41

ANALYZING THE LAODICEAN MIND

If the dispensational interpretation of the messages of Jesus to the seven churches of Asia is correct (Revelation 3:14), and if, as many believe, the evangelical Christians of this generation are God's end-time people, the message to the Laodicean believers should draw our avid interest.

And even if the dispensational approach is not accepted, the letter is still the Word of God and, as such, "is profitable for doctrine, for reproof, for correction, for instruction in righteousness." So it deserves our careful attention.

We are much inclined to the former position, if for no other reason than that the church in our day appears increasingly to display Laodicean characteristics. What qualified observer would contend that more Christians today are "hot" than "cold" or "lukewarm"? Who would argue that we are on a rising tide of blessing and revival, rather than an ebbing tide of diminishing fervor and zeal? Careful statistics and objective investigation would make such contentions utterly untenable.

Awareness of our present location in prophetic fulfillment and recognition of our jeopardy as end-time believers should stimulate us to search the Scriptures to discover God's formula for survival and to take definite personal action to counteract the alarming drift. When God warned Lot of Sodom's impending doom, He gave him the plan for survival: "Escape for thy life; look not behind thee . . . escape to the mountain, lest thou be consumed" (Genesis 19:17).

Another word on survival is found in Jesus' promise to the overcoming church in Philadelphia: "Because thou hast kept the word of my patience, I also will keep thee from the hour of temptation [trial, testing], which shall come upon all the world, to try them that dwell upon the earth" (Revelation 3:10). God always provides a way for His own to escape the judgment that is about to destroy His enemies.

In analyzing the nature of the Laodicean mind we find their spiritual temperature was low. It was subnormal and totally unacceptable to the Head of the Church. In our constant and proper emphasis on the importance of Christian conduct we may fail to recognize and stress the equally vital matter of spiritual fervor.

Jesus found little fault, if any, with the Laodiceans' manner of life. His stern rebuke was aimed at the insipid and lukewarm state of their hearts toward Him. If anyone should consider this a matter of secondary importance, let him notice the severity of the penalty: "I will spew thee out of my mouth" (Revelation 3:16); or, as we would say today, "I will have nothing more to do with you." If persistent lukewarmness in the believer can result in literal excommunication from Christ, how can the gravity of the offense be exaggerated?

Their attitude is revealed in one brief sentence of a dozen words: "I am rich, and increased with goods, and have need of nothing" (Revelation 3:17). By their statement their hearts were laid bare. By their words they were condemned.

The Laodiceans had suffered a total loss of the sense of need. "I have need of nothing." Such an attitude is directly opposite the teaching of Jesus, for He said, "As the branch cannot bear fruit of itself, except it abide in the vine; no more can ye, except ye abide in me. . . . For without me ye can do nothing" (John 15:4, 5).

Today the neglected Bibles, the empty prayer closets, the forsaken altars, and the skimpy attendance at many midweek services all cry in eloquent silence, "I have need of nothing."

44

Another characteristic of the Laodicean mind was a deadly distortion of values. "I am rich, and increased with goods" or, as the Amplified New Testament reads, "I have prospered and grown wealthy." The Laodiceans substituted earthly goods for heavenly riches and equated material property with spiritual prosperity.

In this day of unprecedented church construction, we need to be reminded that the church of Jesus Christ had no church buildings for the first 300 years of its existence. Today we have fine houses of worship and we thank God for them, but we dare not take pride in them. If we stoop to carnal glorying and boasting of our church facilities, we are no better than the pagan Nebuchadnezzar who bragged, "Is not this great Babylon, that I have built ... by the might of my power, and for the honor of my majesty?" (Daniel 4:30). I fear that many a cornerstone that bears the inscription, "Erected to the glory of God," should in the interest of truthfulness be corrected to read, "Erected to the glory of an ambitious pastor," or, "a wealthy member," or, "a prestige-seeking board."

In a letter to me, written the day before his death in July 1966, the beloved Donald Gee stated, "Affluence makes a nation or an individual forget God." This is also true of churches and denominations.

"Riches" and "goods" are inanimate and neutral; in themselves they are neither "good"

45

nor "evil." It is our attitude toward them that determines whether they hurt or help us, whether they bless or curse us.

Self-deception was the fatal quality of the Laodicean mind. How else could their flattering self-image have been so utterly at variance with their true state which, Jesus said, was "wretched, and miserable, and poor, and blind, and naked"? (Revelation 3:17).

Their self-deception was clearly implied by the divine charge that they were "blind." Oh, that we might see ourselves as God sees us! The human capacity for self-deception is universal, as shown by David's earnest prayer so long ago, "Search me, O God, and know my heart; try me, and know my thoughts" (Psalm 139:23); and, "Examine me, O Lord, and prove me; try my reins [motives] and my heart" (Psalm 26:2). Not trusting his own appraisal of himself, David invited God's searching examination.

To think oneself "rich" when actually he is "wretched, and miserable, and poor, and blind, and naked" is indeed a pitiable situation. How fortunate that the message did not stop there. The Great Physician not only diagnosed the sickness but also prescribed the cure. The divine prescription has two parts.

"Buy of me gold tried in the fire, that thou mayest be rich" (Revelation 3:18). Pay the price required to obtain an experience in grace that will stand the test, and you can actually be as rich as you now just think you are.

"Be zealous . . . and repent" (Revelation 3:19). Having assured them that love had prompted His rebuke, the Master instructed them that repentance was the door that would lead them back into His favor.

Repentance cures lukewarmness. As end-time believers this should give us pause to ponder, pray, and let the Spirit analyze your own mind. If we accept the Spirit's diagnosis, let us also submit to the cure of repenting, acknowledging our poverty, and seeking God until we obtain His favor and begin to enjoy the true spiritual riches.

WHY DO CHRISTIANS MISS CHURCH?

Every serious Bible student recognizes that while *all* Scripture has value for God's people of *all ages* of the Church, specific truth is addressed to specific periods. There is such a thing as *end-time truth* specifically addressed to God's *end-time saints*.

Notice the following familiar passages, each obviously addressed to God's last-days people and each containing a pointed exhortation:

"And when these things begin to come to pass, then *look up*, and lift up your heads" (Luke 21:28).

"And he called his ten servants and divided to them ten pounds, and said unto them, *Occupy* till I come (Luke 19:13).

"Then we which are alive and remain shall be caught up together with them in the clouds, to meet the Lord in the air . . . Wherefore *comfort one another* with these words" (1 Thessalonians 4:17, 18).

"And every man that hath this hope in him purifieth himself, even as he is pure" (1 John 3:3).

There is a further word of great significance to the end-time Christian found in Hebrews 10:25: *"Not forsaking the assembling of yourselves together . . . as ye see the day approaching."* Here the subject of Christ's return is plainly linked with the vital matter of church attendance, and by the very association, given great importance. Neglect of God's house has existed in all ages, but this verse of Scripture seems to imply a tragic intensifying of this evil in the end time.

The purpose of this article is neither to condemn nor coerce, neither to intimidate, nor reproach, but to seek an answer to the vital question: *Why Do Christians Miss Church?*

The common and casual excuses are all well known: dislike for the preacher or his preaching; disapproval of the song service or the way the offering is received; the service is too long; too much or too little emphasis on visible manifestations; or "I'm too tired," "It's too far," or, "I'm too busy."

But the real reasons why Christians miss church can be found in three simple words: (1) *concern* (2) *concept* (3) *capacity.*

CONCERN

Concern is defined as "interest in, or care for, any person or thing; regard, solicitude, anxiety."

Concern is interest, as evidenced by the ever-growing attendance at sports events and all places of recreation and entertainment. To paraphrase the Scripture: "Where your treasure is, there will *you* be also." For a born-again Christian to neglect the house of God for lack of interest is inescapably self-incriminating.

Concern is solicitude, by-product of love; and love always seeks the company of the beloved. When true love for God's house and His kingdom fills the believer's heart, every service is anticipated with delight and pleasure. King David, with infinitely less reason, shames us with his frequent rhapsodies on the delights of God's house: "I was glad when they said unto me, Let us go into the house of the Lord"; "For a day in thy courts is better than a thousand"; "Lord, I have loved the habitation of thy house." It can be said with sad and reluctant certainty that *lack of concern* is responsible for thousands of empty church seats across the nation every week.

CONCEPT

Concept is defined as "the image, idea, or notion of any action or thing which is formed in the mind." If the Christian's concept of what

50

a church service really is—or should be—is faulty and unscriptural, it follows that his attitude concerning his attendance will be greatly affected thereby.

Judging by the conduct sometimes seen both inside and outside of churches, it seems that a true New Testament concept of the church is almost totally lacking. For instance, loud talking and boisterous laughter are considered offensive and are universally prohibited in such public places as a library, a hospital, a classroom, or a concert hall. And yet, astonishingly, they are quite commonly found in our churches, both before and after the service! If such practices are repulsive to people of average intelligence and culture, how infinitely more so must they be to the easily grieved Holy Spirit!

The New Testament concept of what a meeting of God's Spirit-filled people should be is clearly outlined in 1 Corinthians 14:23-26. It begins with the *assumption of 100 percent attendance!* "If therefore *the whole church* be come *together into one place.*" "The whole church . . . together . . . one place." What an opportunity for God! We are instantly reminded of the identical conditions on the Day of Pentecost: "They were *all* with one accord *in one place.*"

Paul's ideal meeting involved three distinct goals:

First, he depicted the convicted unbeliever so affected by the service that he ends up "falling down on his face [worshipping] God."

51

Next, he emphasized the unanimous participation of the believers. *"Every one of you hath a part."*

What a far cry from what is commonly found today. The majority of the congregation generally sit as spectators, in varying degrees of boredom and inattention. Many take no part in the singing, the offering, the altar service, and yet they pride themselves on being members in good standing. How unspeakably sad that many of our churches have learned to live without the glory; without the spontaneity of the Spirit; without the divine excitement of spiritual freedom and inspiration. Too often "The Program" has taken the place of all these glorious blessings, once so widespread among us. Sad and futile substitute!

The third phase of Paul's ideal meeting was *the edifying of the saints.* He used words like "edifying" (v. 26) "learn" (v. 31) and "comforted" (v. 21). All these potential and necessary blessings are missed by the absent Christian.

Our concept of the church must include the fact that a true service is a *team effort.* It *demands responsive participation* by all present.

On the morning of D-Day, General Eisenhower said to his officers, "It's *one team*—or we lose!" Imagine the chaos in a game played by a seven-man baseball team, or a three-man basketball team, or a football team with nine men. Imagine any office, factory, school, or army trying to function with half of its personnel absent. Obviously impossible! And yet this is what we are constantly forced to do in our churches.

In a very real and scriptural sense, a meeting of Christians is *like a performing symphony orchestra.* Jesus said, "If two of you agree [harmonize together, together make a symphony] about anything—whatever they shall ask, it will come to pass" (Matthew 18:19, Amplified). In an orchestra *every missing instrument subtracts from the performance.* How much more do absent Christians impoverish and deprive the congregation!

Again, a church service is *a spiritual battlefield,* requiring the presence and faith of every member. The military analogy is perhaps the most widely used of all in the Scriptures. "Put on the whole armor of God." "We wrestle not with flesh and blood, but against principalities and powers." "The weapons of our warfare are mighty through God to the pulling down of strongholds."

When Israel made a war of vengeance on Benjamin, absolute response by every tribe was compulsatory, and *failure to participate* was punished by death! "For they had made a great oath concerning *him that came not up* to the Lord to Mizpeh, saying, He shall surely be put to death" (Judges 21:5). This is not written to advocate a plan of compulsory church attendance, but to illustrate again the ancient maxim, "In union there is strength."

A further example of fatal nonparticipation is found in Numbers 9:13: "That man that *forbeareth to keep the passover*, even the same soul shall be *cut off* from among his people; because *he brought not* the offering of the Lord in his appointed season, *that man shall bear his sin*." How can we assume that the God, who dealt so severely with nonparticipation then, considers it a matter of small importance now?

CAPACITY

Capacity means "the power of receiving and holding ideas, knowledge, etc.; the comprehension of the mind; the receptive faculty; capability of understanding or feeling." Jesus clearly taught that all men have not the same capacity for truth, saying, "He that is *able to receive it*, let him receive it" (Matthew 19:12).

The man with no appreciation for classical music *has no desire* to attend a symphony concert; the artistically ignorant don't enjoy visiting an art gallery. So the shallow Christian, the immature and carnal Christian, the worldly-minded, the spiritually dwarfed and stunted Christian finds no great pleasure in God's house; for his capacity to appreciate, to appropriate, and to understand what he hears is inadequate and undeveloped.

"Strong meat belongeth to them that are of full age [mature], even those who by reason of use, have their senses exercised to discern both good and evil" (Hebrews 5:14). Capacity for food and enjoyment of it is undeniably linked with health and appetite. Healthy people enjoy their meals, and healthy Christians enjoy their meetings.

In searching for the reasons for the deplorable absentee records of many Christians, two added words loom very large. The first is *lethargy*, meaning "drowsiness; continual or profound sleep, from which a person can scarcely be awakened." The second is *apathy*, which is "want of feeling; lack of passion, emotion, or excitement. Always implies insensibility or indifference."

Here we are indeed face-to-face with the real enemies of God's house and God's purposes today. We are not sinful, just sleepy; not wicked, just wordly; not evil, just empty!

DESTRUCTIVE CRITICISM

Matthew Henry, author of the popular commentary on the whole Bible, once said, "The least judicious are the most censorious, and the weak-headed are the most hot-headed."

Perhaps no single forbidden action is more commonly found and casually practiced among Christians than unkind criticism of others. Very possibly its prevalence is itself the major factor that conditions us to accept it. "Everybody does it" becomes the standard justification and rationalization for its presence in our lives.

But this is delusion and self-deception at its worst! For if the Bible teaches anything with unmistakable clarity and scorching emphasis, it is the facts concerning God's view of the use of human speech, especially by Christians.

All sincere believers will agree that one of the first "purges" that God launched in our lives after our entrance into His kingdom was the purifying of our speech. We found the Holy Spirit ever present to check and to convict us of the un-Christian utterance, whether unkind or unclean, whether profane or just slangy. When the prophet Isaiah saw the Lord high and lifted up and heard the unending cry of the seraphim, "Holy, holy, holy, is the Lord of Hosts," his immediate reaction was guilt concerning his speech. "I am a man of unclean lips," he said; and, as previously suggested, he had fallen into careless and unclean speech habits because "everybody does it"; for, he continued, "I dwell in the midst of a people of unclean lips." The low standards of his society had conditioned him to conformity and the familiar evil had corroded his consecration. Equally impressive is the fact that in response to his anguished confession, God immediately provided the remedy, consisting of "a live coal . . . from off the altar" to be laid upon the mouth of the penitent prophet; not upon his head, or his hands, but upon his *mouth*. Surely this graphic bit of personal biography from Isaiah's pen gives us encouragement to believe that God still has the remedy for "unclean lips" today.

Destructive criticism is a perversion of the normal human judgment faculty. There *is* such a thing as *constructive* criticism. Webster defines it thus, "The art of judging with knowledge and propriety of the beauties and faults of works of art or literature, of moral values, etc."

His definition of a "critic" in the positive sense is also illuminating: "One who expresses *a reasoned opinion* on any matter, as a work of art, or a course of conduct, involving a judgment of its value, truth, or righteousness."

That which determines whether criticism is "destructive" or "constructive" is obviously the *motive* of the critic. The former is "usually motivated by jealousy, by a sense of inferiority, by egotism, that would try to lift itself by putting down the other person, to cover faults in oneself by finding fault with others." But *constructive* criticism is *motivated by love* which produces concern for the other person. You love him enough to help him.

It should sober all Christians who claim and feel a special affinity with the Acts of the Apostles to observe in that early Christian society *a total absence of* any carping, critical spirit! When wrong was found to exist in men or situations, they pointed out this wrong in love. It was redemptive, not critical. A minister of unusual dedication has said, "Whenever I get out of touch with Christ, I begin to be critical of others. But when I am in living touch with Christ and therefore filled with love, then that love covers a multitude of sins. I feel sorry for people rather than critical of them."

Destructive criticism *violates the law of love,* for "love worketh no ill to his neighbor." This alone should place it forever outside the sphere of acceptable Christian behavior and reveal the carping critic for what he is, a wilful transgressor of the plain teaching of the Christ, he professes to love; a deliberate violator of what the Epistle of James calls "the royal law" ("Thou shalt love thy neighbor as thyself") ; and an unconscious servant of Satan, for he is ignoring the instruction of Romans 6:13 by "yielding" one of his "members" (the tongue) as an "instrument of unrighteousness unto sin."

When the unity and peace of the Early Church was threatened by the "meat issue" because certain defiant brethren insisted on their right to personal freedom and choice in the matter, Paul's teaching on the subject was summed up in the invocation of "the law of love," saying to the meat eaters, "But if thy brother be grieved with thy meat, now walkest thou not charitably," or, as the Amplified N. T. has it, "You have ceased to be living and conducting yourself by *the standard of love* towards him" (Romans 14:15). The *law of love* was invoked and made the only basis for determining whether the actions and attitudes of the meat eaters was Christian or un-Christian. "If thy brother be grieved" became the sole consideration, which, if conceded, instantly condemned the transgressor.

If, therefore, the wilful "grieving" of my

brother constitutes a clear violation of the law of love, this most certainly would include the "grieving" caused by a caustic tongue.

Unkind criticism is both self-revealing and self-destructive! In view of Jesus insistence that "out of the abundance of the heart, the mouth speaketh," it becomes inescapably clear that the critical Christian betrays himself every time he voices his abrasive opinions of others. He reveals himself as void of Christian love and a victim of his own uncrucified nature. As the "bleating of the sheep and the lowing of the oxen" made King Saul's claim to obedience to God's command appear ridiculous, so does an unkind tongue betray the "mote picker."·

That *a critical Christian destroys himself spiritually* is made abundantly clear in both the Old and New Testaments. On no other subject is the God-given wisdom of Solomon so penetratingly displayed as in his treatment of the inescapable penalties that follow the abuse and misuse of human speech. "There is that speaketh like the piercings of a sword, but the tongue of the wise is health" (Proverbs 12:18). "He that keepeth his mouth keepeth his life; but he that openeth his lips shall have destruction" (Proverbs 13:3). "A wholesome tongue is a tree of life; but perverseness therein is a breach in the spirit" (Proverbs 15:4). "A fool's mouth is his destruction, and his lips are the snare of his soul" (Proverbs 18:7) ; and finally, "Death and life are in the power of the tongue" (Proverbs 18:21).

It is impossible to ponder these passages without noting the repeated use of such vital words as "health," "destruction," "life," and "death," all in relation to human speech. Obviously, then, any Christian who is a chronic critic is actually committing slow spiritual suicide. The confirmation of the New Testament to this fact is equally emphatic. How can any statement possibly be more uncompromisingly explicit than that found in Galatians 5:16, "But if ye bite and devour one another, take heed that ye be not consumed one of another?" The Spirit's use of such words as "devour" and "consumed" establishes beyond question the validity of the above-stated premise: unjust criticism in the Christian is self-destructive!

Can we possibly dismiss this subject as unimportant or marginal in the light of the fact that James devotes one entire chapter in his Epistle to the use and misuse of the believer's tongue? How sweeping and final are his words in rejecting all protestations of superior spirituality or extraordinary devotion on the part of some "who seem to be religious" but fail to "bridle the tongue." Without hesitation the sentence is passed on all such, "This man's religion is vain."

Unkind criticism is flatly and ominously forbidden to the Christian by Jesus, and is therefore the defiant act of a spiritual rebel! Once more we may ask, how can the English language be clearer than in the first five verses of Matthew 7, beginning with the familiar words, "Judge not, that ye be not judged"? The ominous overtones are unmistakable as He continues, "For with what judgment ye judge, ye shall be judged." His scorn for the religious "mote picker" is clearly seen in His opprobious phrase, "Thou hypocrite, first cast out the beam out of thine own eye."

The fact that a critical spirit is not found in mature people would seem to brand it *per se* as a bitter fruit of the carnal nature, and classify it forever with the vile, vicious, and vulgar "works of the flesh" as outlined in Galatians 5.

Think of the most critical person you know and ask yourself concerning them: (1) Are they really happy? (2) Are they spiritually victorious? (3) Are they well liked and respected? (4) Are they a blessing to anyone?

THE MEANING OF THE NEW BIRTH

To the man or woman without Christ, most religious expressions are quite meaningless; and sometimes they are downright confusing. It is a common mistake for preachers and Christian workers to take for granted that sinners can fully understand all of the theological phrases and figures of speech that are so universally used in gospel circles. The fact is that the average sinner is a spiritual illiterate. He often finds himself as confused and puzzled by religious terms as was Nicodemus long ago when Jesus proclaimed to him the New Birth.

Not that it is possible to strip from the New Birth all mystery and wonder, for even Jesus did not attempt to do that. "The wind bloweth where it listeth, . . . so is every one that is born of the Spirit" (John (3:8). But while we cannot tell whence the wind comes or where it goes, we CAN *hear* it and *feel* it and see its *effect*.

Let us examine some of these effects of the Divine Wind in human life and consider some of the meanings of the New Birth.

I

The New Birth removes all *guilt of sin* from the mind and heart, resulting in a *clear* conscience! "How much more shall the blood of Christ . . . purge your conscience from dead works to serve the living God" (Heb. 9:14). The accumulated load of repeated transgressions in the life of the sinner creates an ever-growing pyramid of guilt that becomes in time an unbearable burden. When the penalty for his sin was pronounced upon Cain, he cried with despair, "My punishment is greater than I can bear" (Gen. 4:13). His load of guilt appeared to him intolerable. David also voiced the distress of the sinner when he cried, "For mine iniquities are gone over mine head: as an heavy burden they are too heavy for me" (Psa. 38:4). In a very real sense we are not punished for our sins, so much as by them!

But in the New Birth all this is changed. Only the twice-born can understand the accuracy and the reality of the old hymn, "At the Cross, at the Cross, where I first saw the light, and *the burden of my heart rolled away.*" For that is exactly what happens. The burden of sin is lifted, the heavy heart is made light, and the conscience is made crystal-clear. "The explosive power of a new affection" drives from the life all things of an unworthy nature that formerly enthralled, as thoroughly as the rising sap in the springtime forces from the tree all of last year's dead leaves. The *guilt of sin* is gone!

II

The New Birth also breaks *the power of sin* in the life, making possible *a clean life!* Freedom from sin is promised seven times in a single chapter of Romans. "That the body of sin might be destroyed, that henceforth we should not serve sin" (Rom. 6:6). "Dead indeed unto sin, but alive unto God" (Rom. 6:11). "For sin shall not have dominion over you" (Rom. 6:14). "Being then made free from sin, ye became the servants of righteousness" (Rom. 6:18). These and other verses in Romans 6 sound the glorious note of victory over sin, and constitute God's clear offer of deliverance to "whosoever will."

If the New Birth meant only the pardoning of past transgressions it would fail to meet human need, for the sinful nature with all its evil desires and actions would still be intact. But, thanks be to God, the forgiveness of the past is only *part* of the salvation that Christ

65

offers. "He breaks the *power* of cancelled sin, and sets the prisoner free." Salvation means not moral reformation but moral regeneration. The heart is changed, the desires are purged, the inward thought pattern is broken and recast in conformity with God's will, and the individual is "transformed by the renewing of the mind."

The New Birth also purges *the record of sin* from God's book. That a record of individual sins is kept by God is clearly shown in Rev. 20:12: "And I saw the dead, small and great, stand before God; and *the books were opened* . . . and the dead were judged out of those things which were found written in the books, according to their works." This damning document will silence any and all debate that might arise in protest against the divine verdict of guilty. So detailed and minute is this personal record that it includes not only "deeds" but "words" as well. What else could Jesus have meant when He said, "Every idle word that men shall speak, they shall give account thereof in the day of judgment" (Matt. 12:36). What a compilation of corruption the record of multitudes of sinners must be!

What consternation when long-forgotten deeds of evil and long-buried iniquities are read from God's books to impenitent sinners! What anguish when the unanswerable recital of transgressions is given point-blank to the once-brazen Christ-rejector! But how great is the grace that God extends to *purge the guilty rec-*

ord for all who accept His Son! For this was His promise long before Jesus came—"I have *blotted out* as a thick cloud thy transgressions" (Isa. 44:22). "And their sins and iniquities will I *remember* no more" (Heb. 10:17). This divine "blotting out" and "forgetting" of sin is most assuredly one of the glorious fruits and benefits of the New Birth. .

III

The workings of God in the New Birth are not all negative; they are also positive. Not only does He "take out;" He also "puts in." The born-again person becomes a clean vessel into which God can pour His Spirit, and impart His nature and power.

Jesus said, "No man putteth new wine into old bottles, . . . but new wine must be put into new bottles" (Luke 5:37, 38). This is an obvious reference to the impossibility of putting the Spirit of God into an unsaved life. The New Birth makes us "new bottles" into which God can put the "new wine" of eternal life. The average unsaved person fails to understand this; he has the notion that getting saved is merely getting "right with God," and therefore that it is something that can wait until the end of life. But God's salvation gives *power to live* as well as *peace to die*. Only the twice-born fully understand and experience the life-transforming promise made by God centuries before the Christian era—"Then will I sprinkle clean water upon you, and ye shall be clean: . . .

a new heart also will I give you, and a new spirit will I put within you; and I will take away the stony heart out of your flesh, and I will give you an heart of flesh. And I will put my Spirit within you, and cause you to walk in my statutes" (Ezek. 36:25-27). Here is (1) *purging of the past,* (2) *power for the present, and* (3) *promise for the future!* It is freely offered to all who will accept Christ in the New Birth.

THE DEADLY DEFICIENCY

It is perhaps possible that many of us have never taken a good, straight look at 1 Corinthians 13. If we have, it is most difficult to explain our general attitude toward it, which ranges from lukewarm interest to the casual conclusion that it is unrealistic theology, not practical for twentieth-century living. But neither indifference nor rejection of its valid application to our daily lives can erase its searching language nor nullify our responsibility to walk in its light.

It is as divinely inspired as John 3:16, as inescapable as the law of sowing and reaping. It stands as a mighty tower of light, pointing the Christian to the way of Christlikeness in his daily life. It opens magnificent vistas of a life free from all that is petty and mean and small. It offers the golden key to victory over the misery-laden manifestations of the carnal nature. In the presence of the kind of love it defines and offers, unkindness and envy perish, vanity and pride disappear, self-seeking and greediness wither, and dark moods, temper tantrums, and a vindictive spirit must die, finding nothing on which to feed. It is the love that never fails!

This wondrous word of 1 Corinthians 13 brings to us the heavenly message that we may personally have an experience in grace that will equip and fortify us to meet *anything* that life can bring, for he who possesses and is possessed by this love, bears, believes, hopes, and endures *all things!*

This chapter is God's portrait of a truly mature Christian. For if we are not mature in Christian love we are not fully mature. It is possible to be physically, mentally, and even emotionally mature and yet remain spiritually infantile. It is possible to possess at the same time, great knowledge and a nasty temper; to have developed vast erudition and still be vindictive; to have cultivated adult propensities and tastes and still remain greedy and inconsiderate.

If the foregoing should appear extravagant or subject to question, we need only to look again at the startling language employed by the apostle Paul in his Spirit-inspired effort to awaken the Corinthians, and us, to the peril of ignoring the divine insistence that God's people *must* have this love. He speaks of things that are highly regarded and treasured by all Spirit-baptized people, and then stuns us with the flat declaration that all these gifts and ministries are of value in God's sight only when exercised by a person filled with this holy love. He unhesitatingly warns that though we may exercise certain gifts without having this love, we are "become as sounding brass or a clanging cymbal."

In thus resorting to extremes in illustration the inspired apostle most certainly was not belittling any of the great gifts and ministries he mentioned. Rather, his sole purpose was to exalt to absolute supremacy the gift and practice of love. It is not a question of having one *or* the other gifts or love, but of having both in proper balance and combination. He makes it very clear, however, that if a choice *were* necessary, the possessor of love without gifts would be infinitely better off spiritually than the possessor of gifts without love.

In summing up the emptiness of the life of the loveless Christian (no matter how spectacular his gifts or great his influence or exalted his reputation) the apostle twice uses the word *nothing*. It is difficult to think of another word in the English language that so thoroughly describes utter insignificance. Its only synonyms are mathematical terms such as zero or cipher. And yet, this is the Spirit-chosen word that Paul uses to drive home to our hearts and minds the enormity of our loss and the futility of our labors for God if we lack this love. Since the inexorable penalty for lovelessness is to become nothing, it is indeed a *deadly deficiency,* causing Christians to be "salt without savor," "wells without water," and "clouds without rain."

Consider for a moment the "expulsive power of a new affection." Think of the unlimited tide of blessing that would envelop our churches if 1 Corinthians 13 should suddenly become as important to us as chapters 12 and 14 have always been. What if our ministers were all to preach, explain, and teach this chapter with the same earnestness, conviction, and urgency that has characterized their handling of chapters 12 and 14? Suppose that the seeking and obtaining of the holy treasure of love were given in our Pentecostal churches regarding the gifts of the Spirit! This would most certainly produce scenes such as occurred in the Corinthian church when Paul's letter containing this chapter was publicly read for the very first time anywhere.

Paul describes their reactions in 2 Corinthians 7:11—"For behold this selfsame thing, that ye sorrowed after a godly sort, what carefulness it wrought in you, yea, what clearing of yourselves, yea, what indignation, yea, what fear, yea, what vehement desire, yea, what zeal."

The closing verse of 1 Corinthians 12 and the opening verse of chapter 14 both emphasize the importance of love in the Christian life. "Covet earnestly the best gifts: and yet shew I unto you a more excellent way." "Follow after love and desire spiritual gifts."

WHAT IS WORLDLINESS?

The life of the Christian should be radically different from that of the unsaved man or woman. That is an obvious and basic New Testament truth, taught in chapter after chapter with unfailing clarity and force. The Christian's appearance and activities should mark him as a separated person, one who has renounced worldly standards in favor of Bible standards, one who has taken up his cross to walk in the footsteps of Jesus.

But to think that this separation is to be seen *only* in outward appearance is to accept an incomplete and wholly inadequate definition of worldliness. To imagine that *clothing, cosmetics, jewelry,* and *amusements* are the sole avenues through which worldliness is revealed is to ignore many scriptures that carry the subject into far wider areas and deeper implications.

In apostolic times there were no radios, no television sets, no movies, no night clubs, no public dance halls, and yet worldliness seems to have been a very real problem in the churches. Obviously, then, *worldly conduct is but the product of a worldly spirit.* A Christian can be worldly without ever actually partaking of any practice or activity generally classified as worldly, in the same way that a man can be obsessed with a love for money without actually having any.

Thinking Like the World

To be worldly is *to think like the world.* The Bible says, "Be not conformed to this world, but be ye transformed by the renewing of your mind" (Romans 12:2). Until the mind is renewed, the life will be worldly, for to think like the world means to accept its standard of values, its definition of success, its ideas of the meaning and purpose of life. But Jesus taught clearly that the thinking of the world and the teaching of His kingdom are often in violent disagreement.

Consider, for instance, the contrast between the world's opinion of *greatness* and Christ's. The world points to a king or ruler as the personification of greatness; but Jesus points to a child, and says, in effect: "True greatness is not in birth, family, rank, prestige, wealth, nor fame, but is that quality of man that is best seen in a child if but embryonically."

Again, Jesus exposed the thinking of the world concerning success as utterly false, saying, "A man's life consisteth not in the abundance of the *things* which he possesseth." He gave, in His own life, an unanswerable demonstration of the truth of His teaching; for, although "the Son of Man had not where to lay His head and never "possessed" anything, as far as the record reveals, yet His was a full life of unmatched beauty, unforgettable service, and *success* supreme.

So the Christian must choose—either to conform to *Christ's* pattern of thinking and thus become "spiritually minded, which is *life* and peace"—or to conform to the *world's* philosophies and come to the tragic discovery that "to be carnally minded is *death*" (Romans 8:6).

Living Like the World

Also, worldliness is to *live like the world.* The apostle said, writing to the Ephesian Christians, "In time past ye *walked* according to the course of this world." Unfortunately the past tense of the verb could not be applied to all Christians, for many *continue* to walk according to the course of this world—even after they have professed to be saved. The apostle was certainly referring to worldly Christians when he wrote, in tears, "They are the *enemies* of the cross of Christ . . . who mind *earthly* things" (Philippians 3:18, 19).

Apostolic doctrine as found in the Epistles frequently exhorts us to "put off the old man with his deeds" and to "put on the new man," clearly implying that it is possible for remnants of the old life to be carried over into the new life until such time as the "old man" is definitely discarded.

The apostle Paul flatly charged the Corinthian Christians with being worldly and "walking as men." He based his charge on the evidence supplied by their *conduct*. "You are still worldly," he said. "For with jealousy and quarrels in your midst, are you not worldly, are you not behaving like ordinary men?" (1 Corinthians 3:3, Moffat). Here then is a crystal-clear statement in Scripture that the envious, quarreling and strife-filled Christian is worldly, no matter how carefully he may abstain from certain amusements, cosmetics, jewelry, etc.

Loving the World's Pleasures

Worldliness is such an abomination in God's sight that He declares that the man who is a friend of the world is the *enemy* of God. Notice the strong and startling language used in James 4:4—"Ye *adulterers* and *adulteresses*, know ye not that the friendship of the world is enmity with God? whosoever therefore will be a friend of the world is the enemy of God." Undeniably the apostle here was using the terrible term "adulterers and adulteresses" in a spiritual sense. He was referring to their spiritual unfaithfulness to their heavenly Bridegroom, as evidenced by their response to the wooings of the world.

God is jealous over His people. "What, do you consider this an idle word of scripture?—'He yearns jealously for the spirit he set within us.'" (James 4:5, Moffatt).

Worldliness, then, is a violation of our spiritual betrothal vows. It is flagrant unfaithfulness to our heavenly Bridegroom. It is a transfer of our affections from Christ to the world. In the language of James, it is spiritual adultery. Clearly this thing is a dread malady and a deadly threat to the spiritual life of the Christian. It ought to be rooted out and cast aside with the utmost diligence and thoroughness. To tolerate or encourage any spirit of wordliness is to invite blight and barrenness.

Loving the World's Treasures

Perhaps the most emphatic exhortation concerning wordliness is in First John 2:15—"Love not the world, neither the things that are in the world. If any man love the world, the love of the Father is not in him." When we quote this verse we usually put the emphasis on the first clause—"Love not the world." But God puts equal emphasis on the second clause—"neither the *things* that are in the world." The first clause refers chiefly to the world's *pleasures*. The second refers to its *treasures*.

The snare of the youthful Christian is worldly *pleasures*, but the snare of the older

Christian is worldly *treasures*. The expression, *"things* that are in the world," can apply only to that which is material, such as property, money, and other possessions. Thus the older Christians, who would not dream of going to a theater or wearing cosmetics, are worldly in God's all-revealing light if they "mind earthly things" and if they would be greatly distressed and spiritually shaken at the loss of material possessions.

This article most certainly is not a defense of those practices which we commonly consider worldly, but rather it is an effort to get a more complete Bible definition of this evil, and to show that victory over worldliness involves much more than merely abstaining from certain outward appearances and certain activities. In the light of the scriptures quoted above, it most assuredly behooves the Christian to be sure he knows and understands just what this evil thing really is, lest in his ignorance he unconsciously be a transgressor.

The graphic phrase, "strangers and pilgrims," is found both in Hebrews and in First Peter, suggesting that it may have been used quite commonly by Christians in the early church. In Peter's epistle the phrase is used as a reminder to the saints that they are not "citizens of this world," but are "strangers and pilgrims," and, as such, ought to "abstain from fleshly lusts" or worldly desires "which war against the soul"—that is, which injure or harm the spiritual life. In the Book of Hebrews the same phrase is used as a high compliment to the consecration and separation of the Old Testament saints. They "confessed that they were strangers and pilgrims on the earth," and that confession enabled them to "die in the faith" and to "seek a better country, that is, an heavenly." They were not worldly; they were other-worldly. And, in accordance with their choice of the "heavenly" rather than the "earthly" goal, we are assured that God "hath prepared for them a city" (Hebrews 11:13-16).

To sum up: worldliness is (1) to think like the world, (2) to live like the world, (3) to love the world's pleasures, and (4) to love the world's treasures. But God has provided a complete remedy for this dread malady. He offers to renew the mind, thus breaking the power of world-conformity (Romans 12:2)! and finally, He points to the greatest cure of all: unreserved submission to the cross in daily life and full acceptance of God's authority over us. Then, and only then, can we echo Paul's triumphant song of victory over worldliness: "God forbid that I should glory, save in the cross of our Lord Jesus Christ, *by whom the world is crucified unto me, and I unto the world*" (Galatians 6:14)!

PENTECOSTAL WORSHIP

Of all current fallacies in the religious world, few are farther from Biblical teaching than the often-heard, "I have my own religion," or, "I have my personal preferences in modes of worship."

In fact, the treasured right to worship God according to the dictates of our conscience is a spiritual snare if it misleads individuals to think that conscience is the final arbiter and supreme authority in the matter of worship, rather than what the Bible says.

Jesus' lucid and emphatic talk with the woman at the well (John 4) is sufficient to forever shatter age-old traditions and theories regarding the "how" and "where" of true Christian worship.

NOT RITUALISTIC OR CEREMONIAL

Concerning the "how" Jesus clearly corrected the erroneous idea that God demands *ritual* or *ceremony* as He formerly did in the Old Testament worship. He reduced the subject of worship to two uncompromising conditions: (1) "in spirit," and (2) "in truth," thus rejecting forever all external trappings as essentials to worship. God's interest henceforth would *not* be in holy buildings, holy garments, holy furniture, holy places, or holy water—only in holy *people* with holy *hearts!*

"God is a Spirit: and they that worship him *must* worship him in spirit and in truth." Jesus' use of the word *must* utterly destroys the position of any who today think they are free to choose their form of worship.

In building the Tabernacle for Israel's worship, Moses was stringently charged by God to "make all things according to the pattern showed to thee in the mount" (Hebrews 8:5). He was given no choice whatever in the design or selection of materials or anything else. It had to be built the way God wanted it!

The same sovereign exercise of God's will is seen in His amazingly minute and detailed instructions regarding all the Old Testament sacrificial offerings, whether birds, lambs, or bullocks. To be acceptable to Him they *must* be only such as He had pronounced clean!

WORSHIPING IN SPIRIT AND IN TRUTH

If God was so particular then, how illogical it is for worshipers of the same God today to think He will accept just any approach or will let the worshiper define and determine what constitutes true worship. Rather, logic tells us there *must* be a divinely ordered and approved New Testament worship as surely as there was for the Old Testament era. And this transition is exactly what Jesus explained in the clearest terms to the woman at the well: "The hour cometh, when ye shall *neither* in this mountain, *nor* yet at Jerusalem, worship the Father" (abolition of holy places). "The true worshipers shall worship the Father in spirit and in truth" (the transition from the external to the internal). "They that worship him *must* worship him in spirit and in truth" (the God-imposed standard and criteria).

If the foregoing premise is valid and sound, our immediate concern should be to discover what is meant by worship "in spirit and in truth," and then practice it most diligently.

The Amplified Bible renders John 4:24: "God is a Spirit (a spiritual Being) and those who worship Him must worship Him in spirit and in truth (reality)." Two basic facts emerge here:

SOMETHING DEEPER THAN INTELLECT

(1) God is a spiritual Being, so it follows that our communication with Him in worship

83

must be a *spiritual exercise*. "Deep calleth unto deep"—the depths of the human spirit respond to the infinite deep of the Spirit of God. Though speech may be employed, such worship is more than words. In fact, it may produce times in God's presence when our "understanding is unfruitful," or, "My mind is unproductive" (1 Corinthians 14:14, Amplified), as the Holy Spirit fully possesses the human spirit. If the uninitiated should reject this as sheer mysticism, it is only necessary to point out that the cultured and highly intelligent apostle Paul was its author.

This is certainly not to say that worship is never worship unless it is ecstatic and euphoric, for he who wrote, "I will pray with the spirit," further wrote, "I will pray with the understanding also." The worshiper who measures his worship by the degree of fervor or ecstasy he experiences is in error as much as he who inclines to the opposite extreme in which the understanding or intellect is dominant. In the former, feelings play a major part in worship, while the latter pays little attention to their presence or absence. Paul does not make it a matter of either/or. He plainly sums up the issue by embracing both spirit and understanding as essential to balance in worship.

A WONDERFUL SENSE OF REALITY

(2) The second basic fact seen in Jesus' phrase, "In spirit and in truth," is clarified by the Amplified Bible's use of the word *reality* as

a synonym for *truth*. This would strongly imply Jesus' insistence that worship is not true worship if it leaves the worshiper with a sense of *unreality*. Where does this leave multitudes of church members who month after month and year after year faithfully observe and practice the ritual or ceremony prescribed by their church, yet never feel a soul-satisfying sense of reality in it all?

To this point our consideration has been with personal and private worship. Let us now turn to group or congregational worship.

It is here that objections to Pentecostal worship are most often heard. They generally come from those whose religious background has been conservative or liturgical or whose personal temperament inclines to the reserved or undemonstrative. It is a common human tendency to want to make our personal outlook or experience the norm and standard for others.

REACTING ACCORDING TO INDIVIDUAL TEMPERAMENT

But the New Testament nowhere even hints at a demand for unanimous conformity to a rigid and inflexible pattern of *personal* worship. Apparently the God who gave us differing temperaments stands ready to accept sincere worship *from all*. For while the blessing of God may cause one person to shout aloud, it may be just as rich and deep in another nearby who weeps silently in adoring worship. Recognizing this fact is vitally important. However, accept-

85

ing this truth does not in the least justify the worshiper who is cold and unresponsive, for Jesus' demand for spirit and reality in worship is still binding upon us.

In Paul's authoritative and Spirit-inspired instructions to the Corinthian church on the subject of congregational worship, two phrases seem to be underscored. "When ye come together, *every one of you* hath a psalm, hath a doctrine, hath a tongue. . . . *Let all things be done unto edifying*" (1 Corinthians 14:26).

The first *(every one of you)* clearly teaches what is today termed "audience participation." The second *(Let all things edify)* lays down the final and unchangeable criteria for accepting or rejecting in a meeting the psalm, doctrine, or tongue. "Does it edify?" This becomes the final basis of judgment.

A PLACE FOR "AUDIENCE PARTICIPATION"

Yet strangely enough it is on this point of audience participation that most non-Pentecostal people base their criticism of Pentecostal worship. The victory of tradition over Scripture has been so complete in much of the church world that most people seem ready to assume that the modern church service in which the voice of the minister or priest alone is heard (except for the singing) is the right way. But the above passage from First Corinthians totally disproves this and reveals plainly that a meeting of Spirit-filled Christians in the first decades of the Church was anything but a one-man show! It was a spontaneous and flexible service in which every member of the body functioned and made his contribution to edifying the whole, all under divine control and in divine order.

It is impossible to conceive of the phrase so often heard to describe today's church services —"cut and dried"—as having any validity to Christian worship in those early days. We should remind ourselves often that there is no such thing as a "dry" service; only "dry" servants!

Admittedly, it is difficult if not impossible for the unsaved, the ill-informed, and the carnal to understand and appreciate Pentecostal worship. The Bible says that spiritual things are foolishness to the natural man (1 Corinthians 2:14).

HOW DID THE FIRST CHRISTIANS WORSHIP?

The apostle Paul seemed aware of this problem when he stood before Felix (Acts 24:14) to defend his faith and his life. He had just heard himself branded by the eloquent Tertullus as "a pestilent fellow," "a mover of sedition," "a ringleader of the sect of the Nazarenes." Paul's reply to the governor was not an attempt to prove his way of worship right and that of his accusers wrong; rather it was a calm and deliberate concession: "This I confess unto thee, that *after the way which they call heresy,* so worship I the God of my fathers."

87

Today also, anyone determined to practice New Testament worship must be ready to accept the stigma of "heretic" and "fanatic" from the traditionalists. But this is a very small price to pay for the deep heart-satisfaction that comes with full obedience to God's Word and total surrender to His Spirit. "For the Father seeketh such!"

FLAME AND FORM

Paul Rees has well said, "Flame without form gives you a volatile discipleship; it easily leads to emotional excesses and fanaticism; but form without flame reduces Christianity to the fastidious properness of a corpse in a casket."

A survey of even the professedly Spirit-filled Christians today would most certainly discover far more "corpses" than "fanatics."

If the unchanging principle, stated by Jesus, that "unto whomsoever much is given, of him shall be much required" is valid and in effect, it follows that we who have received a fullness of the Spirit far beyond that of the average nominal believer are under a sacred obligation to "walk in the Spirit" (Galatians

5:16). Obviously the failure of the Galatian Christians to heed that exhortation prompted Paul's surprised question, "Are you so foolish? having begun in the Spirit, are ye now made perfect by the flesh?"

It would prove of inestimable value for every Pentecostal believer—particularly each minister—to remind himself that this God-blessed movement *began in the Spirit*, as did the Church itself!

When Stephen, the flaming young preacher of the Early Church, was challenged by the hostile enemies of Christ and entered into earnest dispute with them concerning the gospel, the eternal testimony of the Scripture to his effectiveness movingly reports, "And they were not able to resist the wisdom and the spirit by which he spake" (Acts 6:10). Wisdom and spirit; head and heart; intellect and anointing; flame and form! Here, indeed, is set before us the ideal preacher of Christ's gospel! This "they were not able to resist!" Wisdom and spirit—the combination is irresistible!

Even the Old Testament church, with its rigorous observance of ritual and ceremony, experienced times of divine visitation when "the priests could not stand to minister" because of the overpowering intensity of the Spirit's power. On at least one occasion "the glory of the Lord filled the tabernacle. And Moses was not able to enter . . . because the cloud abode thereon, and the glory of the Lord filled the tabernacle" (Exodus 40:34, 35).

How then can we, with far greater light and experience of the Spirit's working, ever be content with less?

In far too many of our Assemblies I believe the attitude on this subject is that of the schoolboy who, when upbraided by his irate father for bringing home a report card filled with F's (for failure), responded, "Please don't feel so badly about this, Dad; I'm adjusted to F's!" How easily we adjust to mere form without flame, to monotonous repetition, to church routine, to the absence of God's presence!

Perhaps one of the Scripture portions most frequently quoted in Pentecostal pulpits is, "Not by might, nor by power, but by my Spirit saith the Lord of hosts." But this can easily become lip service rather than heart-conviction; theory rather than practice. It is one thing for a freezing man to admit he needs a fire; it is something else for him to put forth the effort to gather fuel and to obtain the flame needed to ignite it.

The Pentecostal movement began as a revival movement and *true revival is impossible without the flame!* All history of revival through the centuries declares the fire of God as the common denominator. Whether we look at Savonarola in Florence, Wesley and Whitefield in Great Britain, Evan Roberts in Wales, Goforth in China, or Finney in New England, the story is unchanging! "By my *Spirit,* saith the Lord!"

In John Wesley's *Journal* there is an entry for Sunday, November 25, 1757, written in Everton, England, that deals with the absence of the Spirit's manifestations in the church where they had been in abundant evidence just four months previously. His penetrating analysis and logical conclusions seem most timely and helpful at this present place in our history.

Wrote Wesley: "I observed a remarkable difference, since I was here in Everton before, as to the manner of the work. *None now were in trances; none cried out; none fell down or were convulsed.*

"The danger," he continued, *"was* to regard extraordinary circumstances too much, such as outcries, convulsions, visions, trances; as if they were essential to the inward work, so that it could not go on without them. Perhaps the danger *is* to regard them too little, to condemn them altogether, to imagine they had nothing of God in them and were a hindrance to the work.

"Whereas the truth is: (1) God suddenly and strongly convinced many that they were lost sinners; the natural consequences whereof were sudden outcries and strong bodily convulsions; (2) to strengthen and encourage them that believed, and to make His work more apparent, He favored several of them with divine dreams, others with trances and visions; (3) in some of these instances, after a time, nature mixed with grace; (4) Satan likewise mimicked the work of God in order to discredit it; and yet it is not wise to give up this part any more than to give up the whole."

What factors produce a state of coldness and general indifference to the Holy Spirit's manifest presence and power in an Assembly? Does a carnal desire for popular approval by a godless public prompt some to quench the Spirit? To do so is the sheerest folly and fallacy in the light of Christ's plain prediction, "Ye shall be hated of all men for my name's sake" (Matthew 10:22).

Has the related fear of being branded "fanatics" influenced some ministers among us to prohibit all public exercise of the gifts of the Spirit on the erroneous assumption that such things repel and offend the sinner? The apostle Paul certainly didn't think so according to his exhortation to the Corinthian church! "But if all prophesy," he wrote, "and *there come in one that believeth not . . . he is convinced of all, he is judged of all;* and thus are the secrets of his heart made manifest; and *so falling down on his face* he will worship God, *and report that God is in you of a truth"* (1 Corinthians 14:24, 25).

A further factor contributing to empty *form* without *flame* is that certain pastors and evangelists have themselves become negative and even cynical regarding the reality of the evidences of God's power and have persuaded their congregations to accept and adopt their views. Often this attitude is simply a device to cover up one's own deadness and lack of anointing.

Armin Gesswein, director of the Revival Prayer Fellowship, writes: "The Book of Revelation makes it clear that the pastor, rather than the evangelist, is the key to church revivals (Revelation 1:20). He is to have an ear and to hear. If he gets the message, the church will get it. He is God's channel. If he does not hear and heed the message, the local church has little chance, no matter how many men are brought in from without. When pastors pray much, their people will pray. When pastors repent, their congregations will do likewise. When pastors are revived and preach with new anointing, their people will be revived."

The following impassioned statement by Billy Graham should strike a responsive chord in all our hearts. "In an age which is given over to cynicism, coldness, and doubt, and in which the fire and warmth of God is conspicuous for its absence in the world, my heartcry is, *Let the fire fall!*'

"In a day when church membership, to the average individual, is little more than a passing social obligation and the revival fires are at a low ebb, my earnest prayer to God is *Let the fire fall!*'

"In an era when men's hearts are failing them for fear of future calamities and world problems are staggering the minds of our greatest diplomats, the prayer of the Christian must be, *Let the fire fall!*' "